the little green monster: cancer magic!

WRITTEN BY SHARON CHAPPELL . ILLUSTRATED BY JACKIE GORMAN

KINGERY PRINTING COMPANY . USA . 2018

The Little Green Monster: Cancer Magic!

Printed by Kingery Printing Company
3012 S. Banker St, Effingham, IL 62401

Book design by Beth Weeks, www.bethweeksdesign.com

Library of Congress Cataloging-in-Publication Data 2018911404

Chappell, Sharon.

The Little Green Monster: Cancer Magic! by Sharon Chappell; illustrated by Jackie Gorman
    Summary: Whimsical illustrations and poetic text comprise this inspiring family story of healing through science and imagination written by a breast cancer survivor. The little green monster helps a girl and her family survive and thrive through her mother's cancer treatment by providing companionship and emotional well-being during this difficult time.

ISBN 978-0-9997109-7-5

Manufactured in Effingham, IL, USA

Dedicated to Gillian, my heart and inspiration.

when they became very sick.

The little green monster wrapped a special spell around people with cancer.

He knew that sometimes life could be hard.

So, the little green monster brought us under his wing...

and carried us through starry skies and sweet dreams.

His song **helped us face** our fears!

We loved the little green monster so much...

especially his **silly** tricks and dances.

And the

magic that sprang

from his clawed feet.

and medicine that changed my body.

The little green monster

understands all our feelings.

He helps
us surf our
sadness and land safely
on the beach

where the waves

tickle our toes

and imaginations!

many...

many...
+ HOSPITAL

All with the help of the little **green** monster.

Cancer Vocabulary

You may hear these words when people talk about cancer:

blood draw: the removal of sample blood for testing

biopsy: the removal of sample tissue from a mass or lump for testing

cancer: a group of related diseases in which cells grow and divide uncontrollably and quickly

cancer cells: cells that grow and divide uncontrollably and quickly, forming unwanted masses and making someone sick

cells: the building blocks of the human body

chemotherapy: the use of special medicines to attack cancerous cells

IV: the process for delivering liquid medicine into the body

oncologist: the doctor who treats patients with cancer

radiation: a therapy used to kill cancer cells and shrink tumors using different types of rays (like X-rays and gamma rays)

side effects: unwanted reactions or effects from medication or treatment

surgery: process used to remove a cancerous tumor

tumor: abnormal body cancerous cells grouped together in a mass or lump

Our Feelings

Living with a disease like cancer comes with a range of emotions.

How are you feeling?

 excited

 happy

 loving

 silly

 peaceful

 frustrated

 lonely

 sad

 scared

 afraid

 angry

 surprised

 worried

 confused

Little Green Monster Activities!

1. Make Your Own Little Monster

Pick your favorite animal.

Use blank paper and crayons, markers, or colored pencils (or cut-out construction paper shapes and glue).

Draw or collage a monster from your favorite animal.

Use the animal's body shape and parts as the base. Add extra magical features.

Draw the monster in the middle of a magical activity.

You might include yourself and/or your family in the picture.

You can have your monster associated with a feeling.

2. Sing with the Little Green Monster

Here is the song that the Little Green Monster wraps around Marie and her family as they dance in the book. Sing the song out loud. Make your own tune! Do a little dance. Then write your own song for the little monster you designed.

Joyful, joyful	*Fly, fly, fly, squawk*	*Joyful, joyful*
Melancholy, melancholy	*Hold and heal*	*Melancholy, melancholy*
old and new	*Fly, fly, fly, squawk*	*old and new*
a bird's eye view	*Hold and heal*	*a bird's eye view*

3. Paint Your Feelings

Gather paper, tempera paint, brushes, paper towels, and a cup of water.

Put on some music with different moods.

Talk about how the music makes you feel, then paint your feelings while listening to each song.

Try using lines, shapes and colors to express your feeling during each piece of music.

Later, talk about the different paintings you made and the emotions you felt as you painted.

You can use the "Our Feelings" page in this book to help identify your feelings.

You can talk about how you feel during the different phases of cancer treatment your family is experiencing.

4. Make a Strong Container

Select a container (like a shoe box or a basket).

Cover the outside with images of yourself, such as doing things you like or being strong.

Write feelings and words you you are experiencing during cancer treatment.

Fold them or roll them.

Deposit them in the container.

Because our feelings and experiences change, add more words any time you like.

5. Write a Letter to Someone You Love Who Has Cancer

Dear _____ ,

I just want you to know...

One thing that scares me is....

I really like when you...

Something I've been wanting to tell you is...

I don't really like when...

Most importantly, you should know that...

Who is the Little Green Monster?

He could be an imaginary friend.

He could be a bird with extra joyous feathers!

He is yours, mine, ours.

The question, "Who is the little green monster?" is up to you to answer. What we do know is that imagination, love and family are in the little green monster's heart.

We also know that he was inspired by Zoe, the author's rescued Senegal Parrot, who is a wizard at holding things with his three (instead of four) toes.

Meet the Monster Makers

Sharon Chappell is the author of *The Little Green Monster Cancer Magic!*. She is being treated for breast cancer by Kaiser Permanente Orange County. Sharon's first experience with cancer was her father's lymphoma when she was seven. This cancer led to her father's chronic illnesses throughout her life until his death from brain cancer in 2017. Sharon was diagnosed with breast cancer three days prior to his passing. Needing healing, beautiful literature to share with her passionate eleven year old daughter inspired this book. Sharon is also a professor in teacher education at California State University, Fullerton.

Jackie Gorman is the illustrator of *The Little Green Monster Cancer Magic!*. She is a digital arts major at Chapman University with a minor in game development. She was born in Auckland, New Zealand and was raised on Maui, Hawai`i. She is proud of her Japanese, Chinese, Portuguese, Hawaiian, German, and Irish heritage. Her ultimate career goal is to open an animation studio on Maui and share fascinating stories of Polynesia through animated films.

Beth Weeks is the designer who worked with Sharon's story and Jackie's art to put it all together. She is a design consultant and design instructor at San Diego State University. Beth is honored to support Sharon through this challenging time and proud of her niece for facing her cancer with courage, strength, love and a desire to encourage young people who share in her struggle.

May this book bring you happiness during difficult times.

Resources

Susan G. Komen Orange County
Meeting the most critical needs in our communities and investing in breakthrough research to prevent and cure breast cancer.
https://komenoc.org/

American Cancer Society: *Children and Cancer*
https://www.cancer.org/treatment/children-and-cancer/

American Cancer Society: *Helping Children When a Family Member Has Cancer*
https://www.cancer.org/treatment/children-and-cancer/when-a-family-member-has-cancer.html

American Cancer Society: (2003). *Because... someone I love has cancer: Kids' activity book.*

National Cancer Institute: Patient Education Publications
https://www.cancer.gov/publications/patient-education/

Simms/Mann UCLA Center for Integrative Oncology
http://www.simmsmanncenter.ucla.edu/index.php/resources/articles-from-the-director/when-a-parent-has-cancer-taking-care-of-the-children/

FIND US AT WWW.LITTLEGREENMONSTER.ORG